TICKLED
TO BE
ALIVE!

LIFE AFFIRMATIONS IN RHYME

By

JONNIE ELAM-WILLIAMS

CONTENTS

PREFACE

Tickled to Be Alive, my first book, shows how happy I am that God created me and gave me a life to enjoy in an abundant way. People who know me can attest that I use this phrase most of the time when asked how I am doing. It is a statement that gives great joy and happiness to me, and often to others, and in addition to getting a smile, the use of that phrase has initiated some interesting conversations. This has occurred so often that it prompted me to write this book using my favorite phrase, "Tickled to Be Alive" as the title.

Most of us will forever remember the year 2020 due to the devastating effects of the coronavirus, also known as COVID-19. Since the first quarter of 2020, the whole world has been negatively affected in some way. Despite the dismal outlook, I choose to look at the brighter side. There is a great need for things like love, hope, encouragement, and spiritual inspiration. As a believer in Christ, I know that all things work together for the good of those who love God according to His purpose (Romans 8:28); and all things can be done through Christ who strengthens us (Philippians 4:13). So, after procrastinating for such a long time, I decided what better time than during the 2020 pandemic, to finally put together many of the poems that I have penned about life lessons. I believe that spiritual and Biblical thinking illuminates our paths and helps us enjoy the bountiful life that God has promised.

God anointed me with the gift of poetry, and for the past thirty years, I have been writing personalized poetry for birthdays, anniversaries, weddings, funeral services, holidays, and other special occasions or events, as requested. Tickled to Be Alive is a book which contains some life lessons and positive affirmations in rhyme. It is my hope that it brightens your day, along with helping you to recognize and appreciate the goodness and many blessings of God. I am so very thankful and grateful for this opportunity.

INTRODUCTION

As indicated in the preface, Tickled to Be Alive is a book of poems and positive spiritual affirmations that focus on God, our creator, and how much He blesses and loves us and wants us to live a life of joy and abundance. It also contains a small collection of poems that I wrote many years ago regarding our rich Black history. Whether you are reading this book cover to cover or just glancing through it, it is my hope that you will find at least one poem or affirmation that resonates with you. Hopefully, they will enlighten, inspire, or uplift you and make you think positively, realistically, and spiritually about how you carry yourself or handle things of this life.

Life is an awesome and glorious gift from God. He should be the head of our lives and at the center of our hearts. As it says in Proverbs 3:5–6," Trust in the Lord with all thine heart; and lean not unto thine own understanding. In all thy ways, acknowledge him and he shall direct thy paths." If we do this and form an intimate relationship with Him, He will direct our path. Each day, we should enter His presence with thanksgiving, prayer requests, and our concerns. Although He already knows everything there is to know about us, doing this builds trust and a solid foundation. It gives us strength and joy to make it through the day, as well as thankfulness for His grace and the many blessings that He provides. Practicing this daily will make life more meaningful and satisfying as we travel toward our ultimate goal: The Gates of Glory!

Another priceless gift God gave us is the Bible. This is the tool He provides for us to use in every aspect of our lives. As it

says in 2 Timothy 3:16," All Scripture is given by inspiration of God, and is profitable for doctrine, for reproof, for correction, for instruction in righteousness." God speaks to us through His Holy Word. It is filled with instruction and wisdom. Life is a whole lot simpler and more enjoyable if we follow God's word.

Be thankful to God and use His gifts wisely while we still have time. Tomorrow may be too late.

ACKNOWLEDGEMENTS

I dedicate this book to my mother and father, John and Magdeline Dunmore, who both have gone on to eternal glory. Particularly, this is for my mother, who was a strong, spiritual woman; she made sure that my brother, Warren, and I had a strong Biblical background from birth and through our young adult years.

Secondly, I dedicate this book to my beautiful family – my son, Jason, his lovely wife, Mariel, and their children, my grandchildren – Sabrina, Gabriella, and Julian – who all have blessed my life immensely. They are another reason I have written this book, leaving a major part of my legacy, and outlining key points on how to live a plentiful life.

I am thankful to my husband, Elijah Williams, the love of my life, who has been incredibly supportive throughout this endeavor.

I also would be remiss if I did not mention how thankful and grateful I am for all the godly friends and associates God has placed in my life who gave me the inspiration and encouragement I needed to carry out this endeavor. The writing of this book would not have been possible without their love and support, which are very much appreciated.

Last, but not least, I also acknowledge the help of my writing coach, Joseph McCray, an experienced author and owner of McCray Lectures, LLC. I am so blessed and thankful for his sharing massive amounts of information and inspiring me to forge ahead and fulfill my purpose.

TICKLED TO BE ALIVE, PART I

Tickled to be alive! How does that make you feel?
My goal is to put a smile on your face.
Now that's the real deal!
That saying just comes natural to me
— it rolls right off my tongue.
It makes the atmosphere happy and keeps me feeling young.
Not that I'm always so fantastically
happy but let me keep it real.
I have so much to be thankful for;
I just want to display my zeal.

To start, God has blessed me in so many ways!
He's kept me healthy, at peace, and has given me long days.
He unconditionally loves and protects
me. He provides all my needs.
He is forgiving, especially when I confess and
repent – He really isn't so hard to please.

He asks that we love Him and others,
share and obey His WORD—
Believe and have faith, for He is the best we've ever heard.
He gives us gifts of grace and mercy on a daily basis.
He is everywhere, all-knowing, and
powerful. He can be our oasis.

Call on Him. He wants to hear from you.
Include Him in all you think, say, and do.
Try Him — you'll like Him, and that is no jive.
You too will be saying, "I'M TICKLED TO BE ALIVE!"

CHAPTER ONE

TICKLED TO BE ALIVE ...

OUR GOD

FATHER   SON   HOLY SPIRIT

(GOD IS AND GOD DOES – THINK ON THESE THINGS!)

King of Kings	Resurrection and the Life	Unconditionally Loves
The Door/Gate	Prince of Peace	Alpha and Omega
Miracle Worker	Savior	Eternal Life
The Truth	Servant	The Way
Forgiving	Faithful	Living Water
The Bread of Life	Comforter	Restorer
Strengthens	Provider	Shield
Rock/Solid Foundation	Hope	Guides
Never Leaves nor Forsakes	Light of the World	Protects
The Vine	Helper	Stronghold
Shelter	Healer	Victorious
Deliverer	All Sufficient/Is Enough	Mediator
Advocate	Shepherd	Redeemer
Omnipresent	Omnipotent	Omniscient
Peaceful	Blesses	Illuminator
Compassionate	Merciful	Dispenses Grace
Way Maker	Patient	Friend
Promise Keeper	Creator	Planner for All
Sinless	Perfect	In Control

WHO HE IS

Here are some affirmative statements about God.
Hopefully, they'll get your approving nod.

He is the Trinity – the Father, Holy Spirit,
and Jesus Christ, the son!
He is all-knowing, everywhere, and powerful – all in one.
God, the creator of heaven and earth,
He is a King, ever since birth.
He is the beginning, and He is the end.
He is the Master on whom we depend.
He made man and all creatures with His own hands—
And did it all in a six-day time span.
He is imperially powerful and knows everything.
He is merciful and sinless. He is the King of Kings!
He has a plan for all and is the God of Love.
He protects and watches over us from heaven above.
He died on the cross for all our sins.
If you believe and have faith, you will always win.
Read and obey His WORD in your daily living.
Confess your sins, repent, and He will be forgiving.
If you feel lonely, remember, He is always there.
He comforts and strengthens and shows how much He cares.
He has been a servant and wants you to serve others.
Honor the elderly, your father and mother.
He gives wisdom and helps you get things done—
And protects you from the evil one.
He guides, blesses, and does lots of uplifting.
Nothing is beyond His reach – just keep on trusting.

As you journey through life doing your deeds,
Remember our Lord and Savior can address all your needs.

JESUS "I AM" STATEMENTS OF JOHN

I AM THE BREAD OF LIFE John 6:35, 48, 51	Going through Jesus, you will never spiritually hunger or thirst… Believe and trust in Him. Keep Him first!
I AM THE LIGHT OF THE WORLD John 8:12	Jesus will give you the light of life… He will make a way for you when you go through strife!
I AM THE DOOR/GATE John 10:7 & 9	Jesus is the gate to the Father; there is no other way… Accept His gift of salvation – do it today!
I AM THE GOOD SHEPHERD John 10:11 & 14	He recognizes and protects us all the way, to the end… We know, on Him, we can always depend!
I AM THE RESURRECTION AND THE LIFE John 11:25–26	He died but rose and still lives... Believing in Him, we will follow suit, for He continually gives!
I AM THE WAY, THE TRUTH, AND THE LIFE John 14:6	You cannot get to the Father except through HIM… So follow Him. Believe in His truth – don't let your light go dim!
I AM THE VINE John 15:1 & 5	Stay connected to Him; we are the branches… Without Him, there are no other chances!

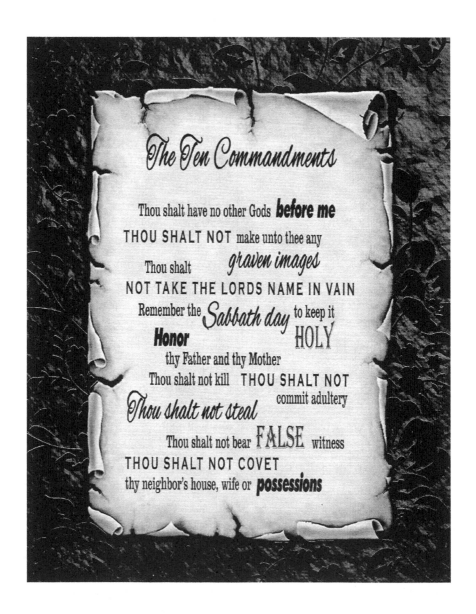

TEN COMMANDMENTS

1.THOU SHALT HAVE NO OTHER GODS BEFORE ME.
I want to be first and "the only" – that is how it shall be!

**2. THOU SHALT NOT MAKE UNTO
THEE ANY GRAVEN IMAGES.**
For worshipping idols, people, or stuff
will keep you in "ditches'!

3. THOU SHALT NOT TAKE THE LORD'S NAME IN VAIN.
Because, if you do, it will surely cause you pain!

4. REMEMBER THE SABBATH DAY TO KEEP IT HOLY.
Praise and worship God. give him all the glory!

5. HONOR THY FATHER AND THY MOTHER.
And always love your sister and brother!

6. THOU SHALT NOT KILL.
Let your anger subside and Be Still!

7. THOU SHALT NOT COMMIT ADULTERY.
That can often lead to lots of trickery!

8. THOU SHALT NOT STEAL.
Regardless of what you want and how you feel!

9. THOU SHALT NOT BEAR FALSE WITNESS.
When you lie, that is not God's business!

**10. THOU SHALT NOT COVET THY
NEIGHBOR'S POSSESSION.**
Practicing these things may keep you from going to heaven!

Follow these commandments and you will see
How much easier and happier your life will be.
In addition, God will be pleased with you
And will bless you in all you think, say, and do!

I LOVE YOU

I - I AM, our eternal God, the Father. We must worship in spirit and in truth.

L - Love God, yourself, and others.

O - Omnipotent, Omnipresent, and Omniscient – God is powerful, everywhere, and wise.

V - Victorious over any spiritual enemies (sin, bad habits, addictions, negative emotions, etc.).

E - Encourage and Edify your fellow man/woman.

Y - Yahweh. Say Yes to the Almighty Lord Jehovah!

O - Oneness – One Lord, One Faith, One Baptism. We are all one.

U - Unity – being of one mind, one faith, and on one accord.

I LOVE YOU – three of the most powerful words to say.
They certainly can uplift and brighten anyone's day.
So do your part.
Open your heart.
Whether Eros or Agape love,
Do as commanded from above.
Remember how Jesus showed love from beginning to end,
Never forsaking us, always a lifelong friend.
Spread a little love today.
Go ahead and do it God's way!

YOUR SPIRITUAL GIFTS

Do you know that you have a spiritual gift?
They can certainly give us a lift.
Once we receive the gift of salvation,
God generously gives us special talents
to share with the nation.
Check out Romans and I Corinthians, twelfth chapters.
Pray and ask God how to use yours in many matters.
We are all unique and wonderfully made.
God has a plan for each of us – don't be afraid!
If we ask the Lord for directions,
He will give us divine instructions.
Think about all He has done for you.
Spread that joy to others too.
God's light is shining from within.
So, stop procrastinating and just begin.
Spread love, compassion, encouragement, and serve—
Teach, lead, heal, be hospitable, for others deserve.
Everyone has different talents.
Discover yours and then learn to use it in balance.
Stop keeping your gifts to yourself.
Share your faith, wisdom, and mercy with someone else.
You will be amazed how good you and they will feel.
So, get moving! Share your spiritual gifts with zeal!

giving hospitality leadership discernment knowledge teaching pastor wisdom administration apostle evangelism faith prophecy exhortation tongues healing miracles mercy service helps

THIS WORLD AND OUR GOD

What is going on in this sinful, fallen plain?
Can we survive all the evil and madness that reigns?
The world looks like it is spinning out of control.
It's like Satan is trying to get a permanent hold.
Wicked leaders, lawlessness, police brutality, and crime in the
    streets—
Dysfunctional families, sexual immorality, and improper social
    media tweets—
Self-absorption, false accusations, civil and social unrest—
Pandemics, sickness, and deaths – some say it is only a test!
These are just a few of the troublesome subjects that come to
    mind.
Keep the faith and hope alive – don't feel like you're in a bind.
Darkness may surround us, but God is awesomely large.
Regardless of how it seems, He is still in charge.
Keep God first, and He will show you the way to go.
He will provide and protect you and give you all you need to
    know.
Be prayerful and thankful; serve Him and strive to do His will.
Stay close to Him – He will even let you know when to be still.

Be humble and peaceful, and watch the things you say—
Once those words leave your lips, they can haunt you forever
    and a day.
Beware of the Evil One and watch out for destruction and
    distractions.
Staying in God's Word will guide you toward the proper actions.
When you make a mistake, don't give up – keep on forging
    ahead.
Ask for forgiveness and repent – remember it was for you He
    bled!
Doing these things will bless and help you to overcome—
And enjoy life now and forever with our Most High and Holy
    One.

CHAPTER TWO

TICKLED TO BE ALIVE ...

AFFIRMATIONS AND SCRIPTURES

LIFE AFFIRMATIONS IN RHYME

These spiritual affirmations keep us focused on God and His presence that is always with us – loving, protecting, and guiding us. They can uplift and encourage us, make us more joyful, get us moving, make us think or focus, trigger a particular action, lessen depression or anxious feelings, put smiles on our faces, urge us to be more prayerful or grateful, or just ground us. Allow these positive affirmations (or your own) to fill your consciousness, touch your heart, and guide you through your daily activities and spiritual walk. They will put you at peace and help you to operate from a more relaxed state of mind, trusting God all the way.

> These spiritual nuggets can lift you up and make you focus—
>
> or put you back on track, so you don't become explosive.
>
> This list is not made in stone,
>
> So, feel free to make up and add some of your very own.
>
> They might just do the trick
>
> and pick you up a little bit.
>
> Use them throughout the day
>
> or when you are feeling a certain kind of way.

*I am tickled to be alive, and this is no jive... God has been so good to me and keeps me happy as I can be.

*Be a blessing to others whenever you can – and always hold on to God's unchanging hand!

*Learn and live Christian life lessons – then see all of God's blessings.

*Set the tone of your day by seeking HIS face – for that is the best way to run your race.

*Jump start your day the best and only way – by praising our King – for HE is in charge of everything!

*HE is King of Kings and Lord of Lords – following HIM will keep us on one accord!

*Stay away from drama and all kinds of mess; keep focused on God and His Word, and you will be blessed.

*Focus on what is good, and your good will increase – focus on what's bad, and your joy will slowly cease.

*Give the gift of a SMILE – it just might take you or someone else that extra mile.

*Let God's life and light shine through you, so you can bless others too.

*Ask yourself, "On whom can I surely depend?" The answer is JESUS CHRIST, our Savior! Believe and trust in Him!

*Do not worry about man and what he thinks – Believe in, obey, and depend on God, and you will not sink!

*Man looks at outer appearances, but God looks at the heart – so keeping it guarded and nourished with prayer and scripture is how you do your part!

*I thank God for my good health – for that is one of the best kinds of wealth!

*Worry creates an opportunity for the enemy to torment us – but worshipping God makes us focus on His love and the fact that, in Him, we can trust.

*Always have faith in God, even when circumstances indicate lack – for God is always there, and that is an absolute fact!

*Do what you can do – and allow God to handle your burdens for you!

*Remember, mean words can scar – so eliminate them or keep them far!

*When speaking, use kind words or just be silent – you cannot go wrong by letting God be your pilot!

*Rely on JESUS in all that you do – He has many blessings waiting for you!

*God will never leave or forsake us – we depend on Him, believe, and certainly trust!

*Live and love the present. Do not regret the past; focus on God, for only HE will last. Do not dread tomorrow, for that could bring unnecessary sorrow. But celebrate today, thanking God that HE is always with us and is the only way!

*Let worry, problems, and all negativity cease… "Let go and let God" – Release and be at peace!

*HE is creator of this universe vast, a universe that will forever last. And even tiny specks like me will live forever – eternally free!

*Rejoice, sing for joy, and be glad – do not walk around all day looking ugly and mad!

*Do not give the enemy a chance to pounce, for he's just looking for that opportunity to bounce!

*Live, laugh, and love while you still have time – for tomorrow may be too late for you (or someone else) to whine!

*Obey God's WORD, and do your best – leave it up to God to do the rest!

*Sometimes you fall short and negativity seems to mount; remember, God looks at the heart, for that is what counts.

*Search for God with all your heart, and you can surely count on Him to do His part.

*Repent and work on making your sins decrease. Watch God bless you and give you peace.

*Do not try to run from God's view – remember, HE's always waiting to hear from you!

*Keep God a part of every bit of your life, and He will see you through good times and strife.

*Never let your light go dim – leave your worries and concerns with Him.

*Don't you meditate on mess – Focus on God, and be blessed.

*Look to the hills, take a deep breath, and twirl – Do not focus on the chaos of this world.

*Depending on God is good for the soul – Leaning on Him will keep you whole.

*Worry keeps you weighted down – Look and soar upward. Get off the ground.

*God is so worthy of all the praise – Try Him. You'll love Him. Come on, BE AMAZED!

*Do not continue down the wrong path still – Obey, follow God, and stay in His will.

*Think about God's sovereignty and how He reigns – Trust Him and let Him lessen your pains!

*Be encouraged – do not submit to your fears! God will strengthen and comfort you. He'll wipe away your tears.

*God will never leave or forsake you – He's always there. This is one of His promises. Remember, He cares!

*Do not look at past failures, current difficulties, or future fears, but look at our almighty Lord and Savior, who never fails and always hears!

*Thank God for His mercy and grace and all that He gives us to run this race.

*The Lord gives us the ability to do what we need to do – for His grace is sufficient for me and for you!

*Do not be afraid, and don't act frozen – Remember, you are one of His children whom He loves, and you're chosen!

*Share your time, talent, and treasure, and watch God bless you beyond measure.

*Get off your butt and stop procrastinating – Give praises to Him and start celebrating!

*All of us should know who HE is; include Him in every area of your life and in all your biz.

*Not on your things or yourself should you boast, but boast on God and His goodness, for He is the most.

*Don't let the things of this world distract or discourage you, but include the Lord in everything you think, say, and do!

*Look over your life. God has given you a testimony. Don't be selfish or bashful. Go ahead and tell your story!

*We are saved by the grace of God… You are forgiven and have His approving nod!

*Walking with God, you are never alone. He's closer to you than your telephone.

*Accepting Jesus in your life is a must, for He is our Savior and the one to trust!

*Operate in your gift and watch things pleasantly shift!

*When you find yourself in a discouraging situation, turn to God with eager anticipation!

*No matter what the circumstances look like… know that God is there with you if you need to fight!

*Be encouraged and strengthened in the Lord, and know that HE will keep you above board!

*The Lord is there; take refuge in HIM. HE will keep your light from going dim!

*Love and praise God no matter what. There are no ifs, ands, or buts!

*What can you give: the gift of prayer… for that is the answer – anytime, anywhere!

*Let go of your doubt and all your fears, for the Holy Spirit can lift you up and erase your tears!

*We are expressions of God, filled with divine light, life, and love. HE will send His abundant blessings from heaven above.

*Do not be so resistant to change. God's guidance will keep you in the right range.

*Always search for God – He is your treasure. He will bless you beyond measure!

*Knowing and honoring God is our highest treasure. All the other "riches" we have cannot even begin to measure.

*You are prosperous, so look for opportunities to give, share, and serve. Do not always be looking for a handout. Why, you sure have got some nerve!

* Give generously of your treasure, talent, and time, and let others boast about your generosity and how you are so kind!

*Constantly showcase your practice of gratitude. Live without constant complaining or a nasty attitude!

*Be disciplined and self-controlled. Be careful of your fleshly desires, and do not be overly bold!

*Seek oneness, even though we are different… A world like that would be so magnificent!

*Pray to God first. Don't staple HIM to your plans – He's always there, offering His helping hands.

*Do not get so caught up in the moment that you fail to see what really is important.

*God's in the healing business and can make you whole. HIS testimony is one of the best to be told.

*God still can perform miracles right before our eyes… So remain faithful and stay alert so you can hear His cries!

*Affirm "I AM" in all situations. Remove "I can't" when you are addressing obligations.

*Affirm "I AM" when you think about the God in you. That will boost you to do what you set out to do.

*The Lord will hear your cries in your time of trouble – He will reduce those mountains and turn them into rubble.

*God's grace is sufficient for our weaknesses too. He will give us strength and always comes through.

*Turn away from turmoil, anger, and division. Spread love, peace, and unity – make that your mission.

*Do not look down and be depressed – Look up to God and be blessed!

*You reap what you sow… So, act like you know!

*Take your mind off of self. Do something for someone else!

*All these troubling things happening might only be a test. Remember to consult with and follow God because He knows best.

*Stay away from negativity and 'haters' – Also, watch out for the turncoats and traitors.

*Draw closer to God while you still have time, for I can attest He is a good friend of mine.

*Justice in and injustice out. Pray and be directed by God. Don't just pout!

*Don't let the evil one kill your joy. Happily go about your day like a baby with a new toy.

*The truth sets us free. Deception, lies, and conspiracies make people flee.

*As I encounter situations that challenge me, Lord, give me the strength to feel safe as I can be.

*Have faith-filled expectation, and God's goodness will fill you with elation.

*Love is the key – for it binds everything together in perfect harmony.

*Let God's glorious light shine through you, and make many a dream come true.

*God loves you but hates sin. So repent, trust, believe, and begin! It is never too late to start over again; following Him is one sure way to win.

*Stay busy doing right things. Eliminate what the wrong ones bring.

*Lord, show me when to be quiet or speak. I know I can trust the way You teach.

*Put away hatred, jealousy, and bigotry and come together in unity.

*Seek the face of God and His will… He will tell you whether to go or be still.

*We are in one Spirit. So, take responsibility and bear it. Love, pray for, and help one another. We are all in this together as brothers.

*Give thanks and call on Jesus throughout the day – He will answer and show you the way.

*When you do not feel your best, always rely on your faith – for believing and trusting in God is the strongest base.

*Listen, be obedient, and strive to follow His Word – for doing otherwise would be completely absurd.

*Do it His way. He will not lead you astray!

*Pray, obey, and receive God's will. Sometimes, when not quite sure, just be still.

*Continually say, "Thank you, Jesus, for your presence." and you will continually see and feel His essence.

*God is infinitely wise… so lean on Him as you attempt to devise.

*Showcase His glory as you tell your story!

*Relax your tight grip on your wants and desires. Let go and let God. Watch His divine flow transpire.

*With God, move toward greater life, love, and peace. Watch your faith, belief, and trust increase.

*God's unconditional love is always there. So, remember that when you think no one cares.

*No challenge is too big for God. So, stick with Him as on you plod!

*Face each day with faith and do what the Lord saith!

*Trying to have your way all the time brings on frustration. Learn to depend on and follow God in all situations.

*There is abundant joy in God's presence. Always seek Him and enjoy His essence.

*Don't focus on your feelings but follow God's Word – for it will give you the best advice that you have ever heard.

*Expressions of God, we each are one. So let's celebrate our diversity and have some fun!

*The world needs God, love, and you. Pray to God and follow His cue!

*Enjoy life. Be grateful. Stand up and cheer. Show and shout you are tickled to be alive – Make it very clear!

SUGGESTED SCRIPTURAL REFERENCES

Note: These words, phrases, and scriptures are by no means all inclusive. These are just a few of the words and phrases we encounter often, with a sample of the many Bible verses that address them. Reading these suggested scriptural references may help you or encourage you to do additional biblical research.

Abundance	John 10:10; John 16:24; 2 Corinthians 9:8; Psalm 23:5–6; Numbers 6:24–25
Acceptance	1 Timothy 4:4; Proverbs 3:5; 1 Samuel 3:18; Job 2:10; Psalm 100:5
Accepting Christ	John 3:16; Romans 10:9; Acts 2:38
Anger	James 1:19–20; Matthew 5:22; Proverbs 14:29; Proverbs 15:18; Colossians 3:8; Ephesians 4:26–27
Anxiety	Philippians 4:6
Asking God	Matthew 6:8; Matthew 7:7–8; John 15:16; John 16:24; James 5:16; Philippians 4:6; Ephesians 3:20
Attitude	2 Corinthians 13:11; Proverbs 15:13; Matthew 5:12; Philippians 2:5

Being a Blessing	Matthew 5:16; Philippians 2:3–4; Luke 6:31
Bible Study	1 Timothy 4:16; 2 Timothy 3:16; James 1:25; 1 Peter 1:25; 2 Peter 3:18
Bitterness	Ephesians 4:31–32; Romans 12:17; Proverbs 14:10; Luke 6:37
Blessings	Numbers 6:24–25; Psalm 23:1; Psalm 145:9; Proverbs 10:6
Calling Out to God	Psalm 18:6; Psalm 107:28
Caring/ Compassionate	1 Peter 3:8; 1 Peter 5:7; Joel 2:13; Lamentations 3:22–23
Cheerfulness	Proverbs 15:13, 15
Christ's Love	John 3:16; John 10:11; John 15:9, 13; 1 John 4:19
Christian Living	Romans 12:1–2; Ephesians 4:1–6, 26, 31–32; Colossians 3:5–10; 2 Corinthians 5:17; James 1:19–27; Philippians 4:8–9
Complaining	1 Peter 4:9; Philippians 2:14–15; Proverbs 12:16; Proverbs 13:3; James 1:19

Confidence	Hebrews 13:6; Psalm 71:5; Psalm 121:1–2; John 16:33
Contentment	Philippians 4:11; 1 Timothy 6:6
Conscience	1 Timothy 1:5; Acts 24:16; Proverbs 20:5; Hebrews 10:22; Luke 17:21
Counting God's Blessings	Ephesians 1:1–14; Psalm 68:19
Courage/ Courageous	1 Chronicles 28:20; 1 Corinthians 16:13; Philippians 4:13; 2 Timothy 1:7; John 6:20; Isaiah 12:2
Courtesy	Philippians 4:5; 1 Corinthians 11:33; Matthew 7:12; Hebrews 13:2; 1 Peter 3:8
Daily Talks with God	Isaiah 50:4–5; Psalm 119:105; Matthew 24:35; Mark 1:35; 2 Peter 3:18
Decisions	James 1:5; Proverbs 16:1–2, 17
Depending on God	Psalm 9:9; Psalm 18:2; Psalm 55:22; Psalm 56:3–4; Psalm 62:7
Discipleship	Mark 1:17–18; Mark 8:34–35; Ephesians 5:1; Psalm 128:1; John 8:12;
Discipline	1 Timothy 4:7; Colossians 3:23; Proverbs 16:32; Ecclesiastes 7:8; Ephesians 6:10

Disappointments	Psalm 34:19; Psalm 107:13; Psalm 112:7; Psalm 126:5; Psalm 147:3; Hebrews 12:5
Dreams	Acts 2:17; Daniel 1:17; Job 33:14–18
Encouragement	Hebrews 3:13; Hebrews 10:24; 1 Thessalonians 5:11, 14; Galatians 6:2; Ephesians 4:29; Romans 12:8
Enthusiasm	Colossians 3:23; Ephesians 6:7; 1 Thessalonians 5:16
Eternal Life	John 3:16; John 5:24; 1 John 2:17; 1 John 5:11–13; Romans 6:23
Evil/Evildoers	1 Peter 5:8; Ephesians 6:11; James 4:7–8; 3 John 1:11; Psalm 37:1–2, 9
Faith	Hebrews 11; Matthew 17:20; John 20:29; Mark 5:34; 1 Peter 5:9
Faith-Filled Expectation	Psalm 40:1; Ephesians 3:20; Isaiah 30:18
Family	1 Timothy 5:4, 8; Joshua 24:15; Luke 11:17
Fear	Hebrews 13:6; Psalm 23:4; Psalm 27:1
Fellowship	Psalm 133:1; 1 Peter 1:22; 1 John 2:10; Romans 15:7; Colossians 3:14; 1 Corinthians 1:10

Focusing on God	Colossians 3:1–2; Matthew 15:8; Jeremiah 29:13; 2 Timothy 2:15; Matthew 5:44; Matthew 6:24; Ephesians 4:32
Forgiveness	Mark 11:25; Luke 6:37; Matthew 6:12
Friends	1 John 4:11; Proverbs 27:9–10, 17
Fruit of the Spirit	Galatians 5:22–23
Future	Jeremiah 29:11–12; Proverbs 23:18; Proverbs 24:14; Psalm 62:5
Generosity	Matthew 10:8; 2 Corinthians 9:7; Luke 3:11; Acts 20:35; Galatians 6:10
Gifts	Ephesians 2:8–9; Ephesians 4:8; 1 Timothy 4:14; 1 Corinthians 4:4–6; Romans 12:6–8; 1 Peter 4:10–11; James 1:17; Proverbs 18:16
Giving/Offering	2 Corinthians 8:6–8; 1 Chronicles 29:14; Proverbs 3:9; Deuteronomy 26:2; Malachi 3:10; Luke 14:13–14; 2 Corinthians 9:7
Giving Thanks	Ephesians 5:20; Psalm 105:1; Psalm 118:1; 1 Thessalonians 5:16–18; 1 Corinthians 10:31

God First	Exodus 20:3; Matthew 22:37–38; Luke 16:13
God Looking at the Heart	1 Samuel 16:7; Jerimiah 17:10; Proverbs 4:23; Proverbs 21:2; Matthew 5:8; Matthew 6:21; Psalm 44:21; Psalm 51:10; I Kings 8:39; Hebrews 4:12
God's Calling	Ephesians 4:1; 1 Corinthians 7:17; Romans 8:28; Matthew 22:14
God's Children	Psalm 127:3–4; Galatians 3:26; Matthew 19:14
God's Forgiveness	1 John 1:9; Acts 10:43; Luke 6:36; Isaiah 43:25
God's Help	Psalm 121
God's Guidance	Proverbs 3:5–6; Isaiah 50:4–5; Isaiah 64:8; Psalm 32:8; Psalm 143:10
God's Love	John 3:16; 1 John 4:16, 19; Psalm 100:4–5
God's Plan	Jerimiah 29:11; Isaiah 55:8–9; Romans 8:28; Revelation 22
God's Presence	Psalm 16:8; Psalm 23:4; John 16:32; 2 Chronicles 16:9

God's Promises	Isaiah 26:3; Isaiah 41:10; Matthew 11:28; Hebrews 13:5; 1John 1:9
God's Protection	Psalm 23:1–3; Psalm 27:1; Psalm 91:1–16; 2 Samuel 23:2–3; Isaiah 54:17; 2 Thessalonians 3:3
God's Sovereignty	1 Chronicles 29:11; 2 Chronicles 20:6; Job 42:2; Isaiah 46:10; Psalm 47:2; Psalm 121:2; Matthew 19:26; Luke 1:37; 1 Timothy 1:17; Revelation 19:6
God's Sufficiency	2 Corinthians 3:5; 2 Corinthians 12:9; Philippians 4:19
God's Timing	1 Peter 5:6; Ecclesiastes 3:1, 11
God's Will	Psalm 143:10; Ephesians 5:17; 1 Peter 2:15
God's Word	Hebrews 4:12; Matthew 7:24–25; 2 Timothy 3:16; Psalm 119:105
Grace	2 Peter 3:18; Ephesians 2:8; James 4:6
Happiness	Proverbs 3:13; Proverbs 15:13; Proverbs 16:20; Proverbs 17:22, Psalm 37:4
Healing	Isaiah 53:4–5

Heart	Psalm 51:10; 1 Peter 3:4; Mark 7:21–23; Mark 12:30; Romans 10:10; Proverbs 4:22–23
Helping Others	Galatians 6:2, 9–10; Luke 3:11; Proverbs 3:27
Honesty	Exodus 20:6; Proverbs 6:16–19; Proverbs 11:3; Proverbs 12:22; Proverbs 19:1; Colossians 3:9
Hope	Hebrews 6:19; Hebrews 10:23; Lamentations 3:24–26; Proverbs 13:12
Humbleness/ Humility	James 4:6–8,10; 1 Peter 5:6–7; James 4:6; Proverbs 3:34; Matthew 23:12
Idols/False Gods	1 John 5:21; 1 Timothy 2:5; Colossians 3:5; 1 Corinthians 10:14; Exodus 20:3
Jealousy	Proverbs 14:30
Jesus	Hebrews 13:8; John 3:16; John 10:10–11; John 12:46; Romans 8:35, 37
Joy	Psalm 100:1–2; Psalm 118:24; Proverbs 17:22

Judging Others	Luke 6:37; Matthew 7:1–5
Kindness	Matthew 7:12; Ephesians 4:32
Let Go and Let God	Proverbs 16:3; 1 Peter 5:7; Isaiah 55:8–9; Psalm 73:26
Life	Ephesians 4:1; John 6:35; John 11:25; Proverbs 21:21; Matthew 10:39; Psalm 16:11
Listening to God	Psalm 37:7; Psalm 46:10; Isaiah 55:2–3
Live, Love, Laugh	Galatians 5:22; Ecclesiastes 3:4; 1 Corinthians 13:4
Love	1 Corinthians 13:13; John 13:34; 1 John 4:11, 16; 1 Peter 4:8
Love/Harmony	Colossians 3:12–14; Romans 12:16–18; 1 Peter 3:8
Love of Money	Hebrews 13:5
Miracles	Hebrews 2:4; Psalm 77:14; 1 Corinthians 2:9; Mark 10:27
Obedience	Psalm 119:33; James 1:22; 1 John 2:3
Oneness/Unity	Romans 12:5; Philippians 2:2

Opportunities	Galatians 6:10; Isaiah 40:31; Isaiah 43:18–19; 1 Corinthians 2:9
Optimism	Psalm 27:1; Jerimiah 29:11; Romans 8:25; Hebrews 10:23
Past	Isaiah 43:18–19; Philippians 3:13–14; Colossians 3:3; Psalm 51:1–2
Patience	James 1:2–4; Colossians 3:12; Romans 8:25; Proverbs 16:32; Proverbs 19:11; Ecclesiastes 7:8
Peace	Philippians 4:7; John 14:27; John 16:33; Job 22:21
Perseverance	Galatians 6:9; Hebrews 10:36; Hebrews 12:1
Pleasing God	2 Corinthians 5:9; Hebrews 11:6; Psalm 96:8; Colossians 3:23–24
Pleasing People	Galatians 1:10; Proverbs 1:10; Proverbs 29:25; Psalm 118:8; 2 Corinthians 6:14
Praise	Psalm 34:1; Colossians 3:17
Prayer	Philippians 4:6; 1 Thessalonians 5, 17; Colossians 4:2; 1 Timothy 2:1

Pride	Ecclesiastes 7:8; James 4:6; Proverbs 11:2
Reaping What You Sow	Proverbs 11:17; Galatians 6:7; Matthew 7:1–2
Refuge	Joel 3:16; Psalm 9:9; Psalm 46:1
Rejoice	Philippians 4:4; 1 Thessalonians 5:16; Psalm 118:24; Isaiah 61:10
Renewal	2 Corinthians 5:17; Ephesians 4:23–24; 1 Peter 5:10
Rest	Matthew 11:28–29; Isaiah 14:3; Psalm 116:7
Righteousness	Isiah 32:17; 1 John 2:29; 1 John 3:7; 2 Corinthians 5:21; Romans 3:22–26
Salvation	Isaiah 12:2; Romans 10:9–10; Ephesians 2:8–9
Satan/the Enemy/ Evil One	John 10:10; 1 Peter 5:8; 1 John 3:8
Seeking God's Face	1 Chronicles 16:10–11
Service	Matthew 23:11–12; 1 Peter 4:10; 1 Peter 5:2

Sin	1 John 1:8–10; 1 John 15:17; Psalm 5:4; Romans 6:23
Smile	Proverbs 15:13, 30; Psalm 31:16
Spiritual Growth	Romans 12:2; 2 Peter 3:18; Hebrews 6:1; 2 Timothy 1:6
Strength	Psalm 18:32; Psalm 46:1; Philippians 4:13; Isaiah 40:29–31; 2 Corinthians 12:9–10; 1 Chronicles 16:11
Supplying Our Needs	Philippians 4:19; 1 John 5:14–15; Matthew 6:33
Temptation	James 1:13; 1 Corinthians 10:13; Corinthians 15:33; Ephesians 6:11
Testimonials	Psalm 71:15–16; Psalm 22:22; Psalm 35:28; Matthew 10:32; Mark 5:19; Luke 8:39
Thankfulness/ Thanksgiving	Psalm 100:4–5; Colossians 3:17; 1 Thessalonians 5:16–18; Psalm 9:1–2
Think Good Things	Philippians 4:8; Colossians 3:2; Romans 8:6; Romans 12:2
Today/Tomorrow	Psalm 118:24; Hebrews 3:13; Matthew 6:34

Trials/Tribulations	James 1:2–4, 12; Romans 12:12; John 16:33
Trusting God	Psalm 37:3, 5, 39–40; Psalm 56:3–4; Proverbs 3:5–6; Proverbs 29:25; John 14:1
Truth	John 8:32; John 14:6; 1 Timothy 4:7; Psalm 86:11
Virtuous Woman	Proverbs 31:10–31
Waiting on the Lord	Isaiah 40:31
Wisdom	Proverbs 1:7; Proverbs 16:16; Proverbs 13:20; James 1:5; James 3:13, 17
Words	James 1:19, 26; Proverbs 13:3; Proverbs 16:24; Proverbs 18:21; Ephesians 4:29; 1 Peter 3:10
Work	Colossians 3:23; 2 Corinthians 9:6; Proverbs 21:5; Proverbs 22:29; 1 Chronicles 28:20
Worry	Philippians 4:6–7; 1 Peter 5:7; Matthew 6:25–31, 34
Worship	John 4:24; Matthew 18:20; Psalm 89:15; Psalm 100:2–3

YOUR OWN AFFIRMATIONS OR SCRIPTURES

CHAPTER THREE

TICKLED TO BE ALIVE ...

LIVING AN ABUNDANT LIFE

ABUNDANT LIVING

Living an abundant life is everyone's dream.
Is that possible? Is that as hard as it may seems?
Can you really be happy, at peace, and fulfilled?
YES, if you believe, trust in God, and strive to do His will!
That is the main reason why JESUS came!
But beware of Satan, who's always playing his games.
GOD wants us to open the door and let HIM come in.
We are to believe, have faith, and, on Him, depend.
Form a relationship with Him and follow His WORD.
All the Bible's books are awesome, but a favorite is Proverbs.
Follow the guidance of the Holy Spirit
– He won't lead you wrong.
He will keep you on the right path and also keep you strong.

Life is a journey of ups, downs, and many lessons.
But God, through His grace, will send
you some awesome blessings.
Enjoy where you are on the way to where you're going,
But also be mindful of what you are sowing.
Constantly ask yourself, "What would Jesus do?"
For you can impact someone else's life
who may be watching you.
Pray. Love God, yourself, and others.

Show respect and honor your parents, sisters, and brothers.
Eat right. Exercise. Rest, and do lots of positive things.
Be humble. Practice the fruits of the
spirit, and watch what it brings.
Be joyous, not too serious, and don't sweat the small stuff.
Life is short, and death is sure – you can be gone in a puff!
Don't get it twisted. Things won't always be easy,
For the devil is slick and known to be quite "greasy."

So, go on, get started and stop procrastinating.
Use what God has given you – make
the best of your situation.
Remember, HE came that we might
have life and enjoy our lives.
So, give HIM the glory. Look within
and follow those inner vibes!
Put all this into action and don't take more than you're giving.
You too can begin to experience the
feeling of abundant living.

ABUNDANT LIVING INCLUDES ......

Having a relationship with God	Recognizing God, his grace, & his blessings
Loving one another	Being prayerful
Worshipping God	Joyfulness/happiness
Doing your part	Practicing unity
Fearlessness	Comforting others
Being wise	Positivity
Expecting good	Using common sense
Being faithful	Willingness to change for the better
Having a good attitude	Living in peace
Being healthy	Celebrating life
Recognizing life As a gift	Trusting God
Being flexible	Truthfulness
freedom	Living in harmony
Being a role model	Growing spiritually
Soaring	Enjoying nature
Praising God	Being kind
Getting adequate rest	Never giving up
Being balanced	Feeding & helping the homeless
Helping one another	Encouraging & Uplifting others
Feeding the hungry	Prosperity
Recognizing divine order	Responding to God's conviction
Being thankful	gracefulness
Forgiveness	Accepting diversity
Being kind	Sharing your talents
Developing self-control	Teamwork
Being patient	Sharing your testimony
Knowing when to speak/listen	Knowing when to be still
Letting go, letting God	Smiling!

GIVE THANKS

God spared your life one more day.
He didn't have to do it, but He's having His say.
Do you want to find the way to happiness?
Try filling your life with lots of thankfulness!
Focus on the many blessings of God.
That is one way to get HIS approving nod.
If you concentrate on the negative and being mistreated,
That's a sure way to feel dissatisfied and defeated.
Pray for and be thankful for joy and peace,
And watch your strife and heartaches decrease.
God will be your shelter in storms.
Watch how the cover of HIS grace and mercy forms.
Rejoice and be glad that He sends the Holy Spirit your way.
He'll lead and give you the right things to do and say.
Be grateful God has a plan for you.
Stay in His will and wait for your breakthrough.
Thank Him for His unconditional love.
Watch Him shower you with blessings from above.
Thank Him for forgiveness, strength, and health.
Truly count your blessings and recognize all your wealth.

Thank Him for shelter, clothing, and food.
Thank Him continuously and watch your moods.
Thank Him for protection and provision,
For keeping you from division.
Regardless of what the situation may be,
God can restore you and fill you with glee.

So, the next time you are down and begin to pout,
Look toward the hills and give God a shout.
Thank Him for your salvation and HIS WORD—
For it contains the best guidance you've ever heard.
You'll experience the power of thankfulness
And will forever be continually blessed.

*GOD'S WORD	*GOD'S UNCONDITIONAL LOVE	*MY SALVATION
*GOD'S GRACE & MERCY	*THE TRINITY	*GOD'S CONTINUAL POWER
*MY LONG & PRODUCTIVE LIFE	*PEACE	*GOD'S CONTINUAL PRESENCE
*RIGHTEOUSNESS	*GOD'S MIRACULOUS WORKS	*GOD'S MARVELOUS WORKS
*FOOD	*SHELTER	*CLOTHING
*SPIRITUAL DISCERNMENT	*WISDOM	*ABUNDANT LIFE
*COMFORT	*STRENGTH	*ABILITY TO REST & SLEEP
*REASONABLY GOOD HEALTH	*KNOWING FRUIT OF SPIRIT	*JOY & HAPPINESS
*GOD'S PROTECTION	*GOD'S FAITHFUL PROVISION	*GOD'S FORGIVENESS
*THE ABILITY TO PRAY	*MY LOVING FAMILY	*ABILITY & DESIRE TO SERVE
*MY RIGHT & SOUND MIND	*HUMILITY	*GOD, SOURCE OF FAITH

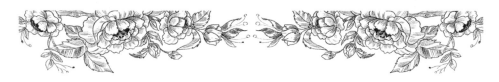

*FREE WILL	*GODLY FRIENDS & ASSOCIATES	*GOD, SOURCE OF BLESSINGS
*CLEAN WATER	*MY CHURCH FAMILY	*AIR & ABILITY TO BREATHE
*LONG GOOD WORK HISTORY	*RETIREMENT	*FINANCES
*USE OF LIMBS AND FACULTIES	*GOD'S DIVINE ORDER	*CONTINUED SPIRITUAL GROWTH
*GOD'S OMNIPRESENCE	*GOD'S OMNIPOTENCE	*GOD'S OMNISCIENCE
*ACCESSIBILITY TO GOD	*MY SPECIAL SENSES	*ANOTHER CHANCE
*DIVINE REVELATION	*THE ABILITY TO LAUGH OFTEN	*DIVINE INHERITANCE
*FREEDOM	*SAFETY	*SECURITY
*TRANSPORTATION	*GOD'S GUIDANCE	*FAITH & HOPE
*TIME	*TALENT	*TREASURE

THESE ARE SOME THINGS THAT I AM
SO THANKFUL TO GOD FOR…

THINK ON THINGS THAT YOU ARE THANKFUL FOR…

SMILE

God loves you – SO SMILE!
That should be enough to bring you from exile.
A smile can brighten someone's day.
It can assist them in finding their way.
A smile can uplift and encourage.
It can help someone who is feeling discouraged.

A smile makes you look more like a friend—
One on whom someone can depend.
A smile is contagious.
Wearing a frown is so outrageous.
A smile can reduce stress.
It also can get you out of a mess!

Don't scare people away with a mean-looking face.
Turn things around and show God's grace.
Never underestimate what a smile can do.
It blesses me, others, and it will bless you too!

WHAT A SMILE CAN DO

Smiling can heighten peace and love,
making you think of heaven above.
Smiling has a power that is hard to explain. It's
not hard to do, and there is so much to gain.
Smiling can make everything all right and
stop you from being so uptight.
Follow the example of a funny clown…
Turn that frown upside down.
You look better when you smile. Try
it if you haven't for a while.
Someone may be carrying a heavy load.
Smiling just might be that special code.
When people are going through that daily grind,
turn that darkness into some bright sunshine.
Someone might be about to give up – or
perhaps some mess is about to erupt.
Your smile might be just the reason for
someone to find a better season.
Erase that tension and remove that frown… and
possibly turn that situation right around.
If you've been feeling down for a while, here's
something you can do – JUST SMILE!
You'll be amazed at what smiling can do. It
can bring joy to others and also to you!

HOW TO BE_____

LOVING	*Jesus shows us how it's done. He wants us to love everyone.
GIVING	*God loves a cheerful giver. Don't be stingy by only giving a sliver.
FAITHFUL	*Don't fall short and go off in a nod, but love, depend on, and trust our almighty God.
PRAYERFUL	*Communicate with God on a daily basis. Pray for others and brighten up their faces.
KIND	*Having a kind spirit will take you far. You'll stand out like a shining star.
COMPASSIONATE	*Do for others, showing you care. Let selfishness be very rare.
PATIENT	*Being impatient makes you come off as mean. No one will want you on their team.
RESPECTFUL	*Treat others the way you wish to be treated. By not doing so, you'll end up defeated.
CHEERFUL/JOYFUL	*No one wants to be around a mean old Scrooge… Strive to be happy and brighten everyone's moods.
THANKFUL/GRATEFUL	*Nothing beats a good attitude. Always display gratitude.

POSITIVE	*Don't be pessimistic, but strive to be optimistic.
TRUTHFUL	*God can't stand a liar. Practicing this will lead you straight to the fire.
HUMBLE	*Don't be prideful. It's unbecoming. Bragging on yourself sends people running.
FORGIVING	*Holding grudges takes too much energy… And it definitely doesn't make God happy.
AT PEACE	*Don't stir up turmoil and lots of drama. Living stress-free keeps you living longer.

JONNIE'S CHALLENGE

Listen up! I have something to say,
For the Lord has brought me from a long way.
I'm at war with the devil, who's ever so busy
Spreading chaos across the cities.
But I will not let him get the best
By striving to overcome his mess.

I love, honor, and believe in God's word,
.Trying to become like the virtuous woman in Proverbs.
Although I encounter life's twists, turns, ups, and downs,
I look to my Blessed Savior, who turns lives around.

So, keep God in your life and live it abundantly.
Let go of the past, anger, and resentment. Live victoriously.
Accept my challenge, and now that I have had my say—
Celebrate God and life each and every day!

PRAY – THAT'S THE WAY!

Praise God and His holy name!
Be thankful and glad that He still reigns.

Praying is the most wonderful thing to do.
You will be amazed at what it can do for you.
It will lift you up when you are down,
And it assures you that God is always around.
It can comfort you when you are sad
And calm you down when you get too mad.

Pray for strength when you feel weak.
Pray to God for that extra tweak.
Praying keeps you in such a good mood
And, along with God's Word, is good spiritual food.

Prayer is a necessity – all should know
To make it part of your life wherever you go.
It is a way to share your appreciation—
Not to mention it improves your communication.
Whenever you don't know what to do or say,
Give God a try and just pray!

A SEASONED VIEW

One of the best things that can happen to you
Is to get a look at things from a seasoned view,
A view filled with wisdom and information
That can address almost any situation.
Consideration as a senior starts around age fifty-five—
Although anyone with interesting life experiences can apply.
Interacting with a senior can be a blessing from God—
For they have much to share from the roads they've trod.
Their many experiences are filled with so much history.
They may even reveal things we consider a mystery.
They can share the amazing, the good, and the bad.
They can leave you neutral, happy, or sad.
They're loaded with all kinds of tips and advice—
Their very own testimonies may even suffice.
They've been up hills and in valleys and endured lots of strife.
They can help you avoid many pitfalls in life.
So, the next time you're filled with "what,"
"where," "who," or "why,"
Give someone with a seasoned view a try.
Remember, our seniors have a lot to say,
And it may just enlighten or brighten your day.

GOD'S LONG VIEW – JUST FOR YOU!

God has a long view of your life.
Your experiences will include some joy and some strife.
But do not worry and do not fret.
With God in your life, you are set.

He has given us gifts and a story—
And wants us to use them to His glory.
First, He has a master plan
For you and everyone in this great land.

Each of us is a unique creation
Unconditionally loved by God in all situations.
Believe, and put your faith and trust in Him.
While traveling life's journey, never let your light go dim.

Talk with God on a daily basis.
He is our refuge – much like an oasis.
Love one another.
Be kind to your sisters and brothers.

Live, speak, and share God's Word.
Be Christlike and soar high like a mighty bird.
Help those who are in need.
Spread peace, joy, and happiness like seeds.

Beware of the devil, who aims to kill, steal, and destroy.
Rebuke him and know that he certainly isn't coy.
He will try his best to stop you in your tracks.
But remember, God will deliver you, and that is a fact.

Regardless of how it seems, God is in control.
Pray, trust, and believe. Then watch. He will not fold.

So now you know what you can do and all about God's long
view for you.

HE KEEPS ON BLESSING ME

I'm so thankful the Lord is blessing me.
He opens doors that I can't even see.
You ask me why I'm so filled with glee.
It's because my Lord just keeps on blessing me.

He wakes me up so I can start my day.
He gives me health so I can make my way.
He opens my eyes so I can plainly see.
I tell you, my Lord just keeps on blessing me.

He clears my head and sharpens my mind.
He shows me how to be oh so kind.
He orders my steps and shows me how to be.
My Lord, My God just keeps on blessing me.

God is great. God is so good.
He takes care of me like He said He would.
I'm going to scream. I'm going to shout
And tell you what my God is all about.

He's merciful, kind, and forgiving.
His BOOK shows us how we should be living.
Form a relationship with Him, and I know you'll agree—
Our God loves and blesses you and me!

POSITIVE PEOPLE

You know what would be pleasing to see?
A world full of positive people, like you and me!
People striving to be imitators of God,
For that is the way to get HIS approving nod.
People going about their daily spiritual walk in love,
Just as God commands from heaven above.
People being positive and full of joy,
Like a young child with a brand-new toy!

When observing others, we should look for what's good,
For God will bless you like HE said He would.
Do your part to make each day great.
Be inspiring and give more than you take.
You'll be surprised at how good you will feel.
It will keep you uplifted and full of zeal.

So instead of complaining and making negative remarks,
Showcase the God in you. HE resides in your heart!

HAPPY AND SINGLE

One of the joys in life is being single.
This allows one to continuously mingle.
Another goal in life is to be happy,
Even though life can sometimes be crappy.
We should strive to focus on the good
And not allow the bad to dictate our mood.
Think about all the good that God has done—
Don't put all your hopes into someone.
I refuse to walk around being sad
Or appear as if I'm always mad.
For God has been just too good to me,
And I plan to be as joyous as I can be,
Whether I have a special person in my life
Or I'm just trying to avoid the many pitfalls and strife.

Remember that God will always see you through.
He will produce many opportunities for you.
If you get down and out about your singleness—
Read or recite this poem, and you might just be blessed.

The next time you begin to feel down,
Always be looking upward bound.
Think of your trials as a little test.
Hand them over to God, and He will do the rest.
Put in your mind this little jingle,
"God loves me, and I am Happy and Single!"

LIVE! LAUGH! LOVE!

Life is a gift, so don't take it for granted.
Don't let it pass you by, then wish that you had it!
Live by the spirit – know and develop each fruit.
Make the best of each day. Don't act
like you don't give a hoot!

Laugh, be joyous – happiness is the name of the game.
Don't take life too seriously or be too tame.
Dance, do something you like, or dare to be different.
Time is so short. Do it while you can still remember it!

Love yourself and one another – one of
God's great commandments!
When you sin or wrong others, practice repentance!
Be thankful and forgiving. Have faith, trust, and believe!
We can always depend on God. He's
got goodness up His sleeve.

So as you walk along your spiritual journey,
remember to live, laugh, and love.
YOU ARE GUARANTEED TO SEE MANY
BLESSINGS FROM ABOVE!

Live Well ❤ Laugh Often ❤ Love Much

CHAPTER FOUR

TICKLED TO BE ALIVE ...

FAMILY

FAMILIES

Family is usually the foundation that gets us started.
They are here from the beginning until we have parted.
Families provide a setting for personal growth.
Families provide love, support, and
sometimes a reason to boast.
Families can supply your physical and spiritual foods
And also can introduce you to various moods.
Immediate family can consist of children, mother, and dad,
But also can include other relatives and
best friends one may have.

Think about the blessings your family brings to you.
Share them with others – differences and similarities too.
Life in some families is just plain fun.
Sadly, some families have problems that seem to weigh a ton.
Whatever your family situation may be,
Stay connected, do your part, and strive
to keep them full of glee.

Families can shape the future of a little boy or girl,
Teaching them to deal with all that goes on in this world.
Remember, children are always watching you
And will often do as you do too.
Give them a strong spiritual foundation
Which will equip them to handle all kinds of situations.
Teach them to love God and self and help out when they can.
Treat others right. Know when and how to take a stand.

Creating a loving, stable family environment
Goes a long way, from childhood to retirement.

GODLY MOTHERS

A godly mother or mother figure is a gift from above.
God shows them how to share their love.
Like Him, they love unconditionally
And care for loved ones unselfishly.
They give of themselves twenty-four seven
And show us how to get to heaven.
They teach you daily right from wrong.
They can often uplift or inspire with the use of a song.
They are supportive, compassionate, and oh so kind.
They have the patience of Job that will just blow your mind!
They're smart, work hard, and make many sacrifices.
The wisdom they display shows why
we consider them the wisest.
Godly mothers often want what's best for others.
They're role models for many, including
their sisters and brothers.
Godly mothers know how to provide and protect.
They think on their feet and know how to project.
Godly mothers hold your hand and provide guidance;
Don't ruffle their feathers, for they can be full of defiance!
Being a mother is no easy task—
They are quite special and the head of their class.
Godly mothers strive to display the Fruit of the Spirit.
You're really blessed if you can attribute these
qualities to your mommy dearest!
So, whether they're still here or gone on to glory,
Reminisce, honor them, and graciously tell their story!

GODLY BLACK FATHERS

Godly black fathers are special and continue to be in need.
They strongly love the Lord and their families,
and do more than just plant their seed.
They are hard workers and know how to provide.
They are smart, compassionate, and oh so wise.
They are innovators and leaders, and know how to teach.
They don't run from their responsibilities but remain in reach.

Godly black fathers are trustworthy, strong,
and know when to be humble.
They are not overly arrogant and know when not to mumble.
They're not always right but willing to
admit when they're wrong.
They know how to smooth things over with a prayer or a song.

Godly black fathers are good mentors,
showing their ability to guide.
Search our history, you will find some
who were "sho'nuf" bona fide.
They strive to be forgiving, selfless, and true—
Trying not to be a know-it-all, but seem
to know just what to do.
They are faithful in serving and helping others,
Being good role models for our sons and brothers.
From the beginning, they're labeled to lead
And most of them try so hard to please.

Often, they are not given the credit they deserve.
So take time to sit back, take note, and observe.
Recognize our godly black men of the
past, present, and time to come.
Let's salute those striving to pattern their lives
after our Most High and Holy One.

OUR CHILDREN AND US

Children, our children are blessings from God to us,
So that is the main reason that we make all the fuss.
So precious, so innocent, so cute and inquisitive…
Oftentimes, they are the main reason that we want to live
As outstanding providers, protectors, and comforters too,
Giving love, guidance, and happiness, to name just a few.
Teach them the way to go from the time they are small,
And be there when they need us and it is their time to fall.
We should show them by example how to live right—
By honoring God and helping others, doing it with delight.
Children are our future, as the famous song says.
And if we invest time in them, we will see, it surely pays.
Enjoy them, have fun with them, and learn from them too—
For all that you taught and showed them
may very well come right back to you.

THOUGHTS ON MARRIAGE

For your consideration, here's a few words of advice—
If you choose to follow them, your
marriage should be quite nice.

Your wedding is a day that you have dreamed of.
If you do right, you will receive many
blessings from heaven above.
Put much thought in the partner you choose.
By following God's guidance, you cannot lose.
Take your time and do not rush into it,
For doing so can cause you both quite a fit!

Take your vows seriously and mean them from your heart.
Love and respect one another, and you're off to a great start.
Put your trust and faith in God, for He'll
keep you safe and secure.
He'll put you on the road to success
and just keep giving you more.
Share and care for each other through good and bad health.
Treat each other the way you would like to be treated yourself.

Communicate and listen!
Give each other special attention.
Remember, there will be good times and bad.
Concentrate on what makes the other glad.
Edify one another and keep others out.
Often they cause trouble and can cause unnecessary doubt.

Forgive each other and don't stay angry for long.
Perhaps you can get over it with the use of a poem or a song.

Through life, there are many ups and downs.
Try to remain upbeat and stay away from wearing frowns.
Don't be too serious – remember to have fun.
Enjoy the rest of your life together, for this is how it's done.

Join one another in marital bliss—
And seal your vows with that special kiss.
Best wishes, for good health, happiness,
love, and peace are sent your way.
Congratulations, and may you forever
cherish your special wedding day!

CHAPTER FIVE

TICKLED TO BE ALIVE ...

OUR HERITAGE/OUR CULTURE

(I wrote these black history poems during the 1990s)

THOUGHTS ON BLACK HISTORY

When I was a very young girl
Growing up in this cold world,
I lacked confidence and had low self-esteem.
I used to think a lot and had many a dream
Of making something of my life
And avoiding the pitfalls and strife
Suffered by folks like my mom and dad
And others before them who'd had it bad.

I was unaware that there were many black role models
In whose footsteps I could follow.
They did not teach about them in school.
No one talked about them, generally as a rule.
But in later years, it has been found out
That black Americans should have lots of clout.

We played a major role in the development of this country.
And most of us come from decent, hard-working, and strong
     families.
So, sit back and listen about the following few
Who have made life a little easier for people like me and you.

Why, there was William A. Lavalette,
Who invented the printing press.
Garret A. Morgan invented the traffic signal and gas mask.
Now, who else but such a talented man could perform such a
     task?

John Albert Burr invented the lawn mower.
Without it, your yard work would be much slower.
The street sweeper was invented by Charles B. Brooks,
Which has had quite an impact on the way our streets look.

Granville T. Woods was the man with the goods!
Why, he invented a device
That made telegraphing quite nice.

We would all be off our block
Without Benjamin Banneker's invention of the clock.
Thomas Jennings invented the dry-cleaning process.
Without his invention, our fineries would be a mess!

Dr. Charles R. Drew was a pioneer of the blood banks.
For his fortitude and persistence, we owe much thanks.
The hot-iron process for straightening hair
Made Madame C. J. Walker's name very dear.

And, last but not least, though I really must cease,
The mother of the Civil Rights Movement — Rosa Parks,
Whose determination to fight injustice became her landmark.
There are many other famous Afro-Americans — too numerous
    to mention.
These are just a few who come to mind. Hopefully, they got
    your attention.
The next time you use an ironing board, range golf tee, or
    shampoo headrest,
Think about the person of color who first put these items to
    the test.

Our contributions are part of history,
And therefore should not be kept a mystery.
Children should see at young, tender ages
The contributions of black Americans included in the history-
book pages.

Now that I am all grown up and learning more each day,
My self-confidence has improved, and I have been inspired in
many ways.
The more I read and hear, the prouder I have become.
It's such an uplifting feeling. I just want to cry out to everyone:

FREE YOUR MIND, OPEN YOUR HEART, AND JOIN IN THE
VICTORY—
COME ON, LET'S ALL CELEBRATE A LITTLE BLACK HISTORY!

PROUD PEOPLE

Should we be proud?
I say, "YES!" Shout out loud.
Black folks have come a long way.
And, Lord willing, we are here to stay!

Brought over to America on ships in shackles,
Stripped of our heritage and constantly tackled,
After years of struggle, we survived our despair
Through determination, perseverance, and lots of prayer.

Many of our ancestors were great Queens and Kings,
And then there were others who invented thousands of things.
Black men and women still withstand plenty of sorrow,
Doing their best to raise our future leaders of tomorrow.

Just think about it – I'm sure you can recall
The names of those who took many falls,
Refusing to succumb to the many obstacles thrown their way,
Overcoming adversities and still having their say.

Should we be proud? Why, I should certainly say so,
But that doesn't mean there's not a long way to go.
Celebrate, but do your part to make a contribution
To the positive struggle of African Americans.

Continue to promote love, peace, and liberty,
Religion, moral values, and dignity,
Goodwill, good cheer, and high self-esteem,
Moving onward and upward with plenty of steam—

Continuously striving for what is just and right,
Keeping God first and foremost in our sight,
Setting an example for our young ones whom we hold dear,
Teaching them to have faith and not to fear.

Sometimes, we may laugh; sometimes, we might cry.
But that shouldn't stop us from holding our heads up high.
Study our history – it is okay to say it loud:
I'M AN AFRICAN AMERICAN. I'M BLACK AND CERTAINLY
    PROUD!

THE EVOLUTION OF BLACK HISTORY

Although there are twelve, one month stands out.
Can you guess which month I am talking about?

February, the second month of the calendar year—
One of the months that, to me, is very dear.
You may ask why and may not understand,
But it should be special to every boy, girl, woman, and man.

February has been designated to showcase Black History.
Unfortunately, in the past, it was quite a mystery.
History books practically ignored the Black population,
Or they were depicted inferiorly with demeaning information.

During the twentieth century, folks
started taking a second look
When Blacks began to gain positive
presence in American history books.
That is quite shameful and certainly was a crime
When you think that Blacks had been in
America since at least colonial times.

Dr. Carter G. Woodson took note and took a stand.
He began to make folks aware of the
contributions of Afro-Americans.
He's labeled the "Father of Black History"
and chose February because
Of the honoring of a few famous men
and the passage of voting laws.

It has grown from celebrating for just one week
To presently Black History Month, now at its peak.

Blacks have excelled in the military and
as inventors and scientists,
And in the areas of education, entertainment,
sports, and even as artists.
They have contributed much to world civilization
And the advancement of mankind,
including today's automation.

Strive to acknowledge their many accomplishments.
Enjoy the many Black History facts that produce astonishment.
The lists keep growing, too numerous to mention.
Many are impressive and starting to gain plenty of attention.

IF A NAYSAYER EVER QUESTIONS,
USING A NEGATIVE SOUND…
TELL THEM BLACK HISTORY IS NEEDED YEAR ROUND.
SO LET US LEARN AND SHARE. WEED
OUT IGNORANCE AND BIGOTRY.

LET'S ALL SPEND SOME TIME
CELEBRATING BLACK HISTORY!

WHY IT'S NECESSARY TO CELEBRATE BLACK HISTORY

You ask that question because you just don't understand.
But think about it——every girl, boy, woman, and man
Needs to be aware of the many contributions Afro—Americans
     have made,
And much thought should be given to all the dues we have
     paid.

Many little children grow up in hopeless situations,
Searching for love and help in desperation.
While others grow up in loving families,
Being taught by their parents to have high self—esteem.

This hard, cold world slaps them in the face,
Throwing many obstacles their way——slowing their pace.
Society constantly tells them they are no good,
While they struggle and fight to gain ground in their neighborhood.

How uplifting for them to know that their forefathers were famous.
How important it is to spread that kind of news — can you
     blame us?
There were many scientists, lawyers, orators, and inventors,
Teachers, activists, artists, and doctors--
Fighting, struggling, and paving the way
For the many young people of today.

Hopefully, all of their work won't be in vain
When thought is given about all of the pain.
So let us weed out the hate, malice, and bigotry.
And let us all spend some time celebrating BLACK HISTORY!

THOUGHTS OF A YOUNG BLACK MAN

(Written for my son when he was age fifteen)

Who am I?

I am a man—a young black man,
Whose forefathers were captured and brought to this land
As slaves, chained and against their will.
Stripped of their humanity, they turned the other cheek still.

But against all odds
And with the help of Almighty God,
Freedom was found.
As the years rolled around.

Strong-willed and courageous men and women,
Because of their faith and dreams, were driven
To make important contributions in this world we live in today,
Gaining respect and acknowledgment along the way.

Even with their accomplishments, I have a long way to go.
Because racism and double standards are still prevalent – you know.
I'll follow their footsteps and make contributions to society,
Keeping in mind the many things I've been taught by those
    close to me.

With God above, I know I won't fail
Because He gives me the love, guidance, and strength I need
    to prevail.
With lots of encouragement and a determination to succeed,
I am certain that I will reach my destiny.

WHAT BLACK HISTORY MEANS TO ME

B - Black is beautiful! What a proud statement!

L - Loving one another is also an essential commitment.

A - Advancement, promoting goodwill to all men,

C - Contributions made by many Afro-Americans.

K - Kings and Queens were our predecessors; their leadership opened many doors.

H - Historical facts fill us with pride,

I - Initiative, ingenuity, and intelligence – things for which we all should strive

S - Survival, an instinctive quality which makes us superior

T - To the many tale-telling white folks who try to make us feel inferior,

O - Observing the marvelous work and inventions of our black-skinned Brothers,

R - Rooting out racism and mistreatment of our fathers and mothers,

Y - Yearning to have everyone all over the land and sea know why

I am so proud, so very proud to be me!

CHAPTER SIX

TICKLED TO BE ALIVE ...

SPECIAL OCCASIONS/HOLIDAYS

MONTHS TO CELEBRATE

Every month has a special time of the year
To take time to give thanks and celebrate with cheer.
So I'm taking a moment or two
To give each month its just due.

January is the first and leader of the pack.
It has thirty-one long, cold, crisp days
with February on its back.

February, though a short month, is for lovers,
And Black History historians come out from under cover.

March blows in strong with weather full of surprise,
While April hovers, waiting for spring to arise,
Washing away the cold and snow, bringing plenty of showers.
May comes along showcasing emeralds and pretty flowers.

June, the first month of summer – how welcome it is!
Then patriotic July on the scene comes quick as a whiz!

Hot, steaming August brings vacations and plenty of fun.
Before you know it, September's here, and summer is done!
Back to work and school – no more loafing on the beach!
Pull out the pencils and the books. The
teachers are ready to teach.

October is a fun fall month – and ends with Halloween—
Ghosts, goblins, and costumed folks are all over the scene.

Fall comes and goes, and Thanksgiving
is celebrated in November.
Jesus' birthday and Christmas are celebrated in December.
The end of the year brings back the cold weather.
For some of us, that might even make things better.

So there – we've made it from beginning to end.
Every month was mentioned, and some
memories might even make you grin.

God knew what He was doing when
these months were formed.
Everyone gets to feel special in the
month that they were born.

I've celebrated and highlighted each
season and month of the year.
Cherish the months and seasons that you hold dear.
Live your life and enjoy it to the max.
It's the only one you've been given, and that's a fact!

CHRISTMAS THOUGHTS

Christmas time is here again.
Helping hands, everyone should lend.
Hustling, bustling, and lots of shopping.
Eating all types of goodies with special toppings.

But wait a minute! What could be missing?
Could it be that we are only thinking about receiving, not giving?
Or have we thought about our dear Christ Savior
Born on Christmas Day in a little manger?

Joseph and Mary had no one on whom to depend.
They were sent to the stables because there was no room at
        the inn.
Good news and great joy were the baby's claim to fame,
And after the passing of several days, JESUS became His name.

Guests came from all over, bearing special gifts.
Just the thought of this story should give us a lift.
So let's not get caught up in the commercialism
Or all the fantasy stories on television.

Let's not forget to remember those who are less fortunate.
Do something to help them – even if it is just a little bit.
Be loving and helpful and spread holiday cheer,
But practice doing this all throughout the year.
Honoring Christ Jesus is a good way to start—
And this season's greeting comes straight from the heart.

YOU ARE DEAR – SPREAD SOME CHEER

The Yuletide season comes only once a year.
Who says that's the only time to spread good cheer?
Christ, our Savior, loves each and every one.
So, let us follow His lead and join in the fun.
Love and help one another each and every day.
Strive to stay positive as you make your way.
Always be thankful and count your blessings.
Learn from your mistakes and your lessons.
You will be surprised at what good all of this will do.
It will inspire and uplift others and do the same for you too!

This Photo by Unknown Author is licensed under CC BY-ND

EASTER THOUGHTS

Do you remember the song "Here comes Peter Cottontail
Hopping down the bunny trail?"
Or what about "In Your Easter Bonnet…
With all the frills upon it?"

But what we should recall
Is the greatest truth of all.
Jesus Christ died on the cross
And suffered the supreme loss.
He died for the sins we commit,
And to the Father, the Son, and the Holy Ghost, we should
submit.

They tortured Him mercilessly until He bled,
And very many tears were shed.
He was hung between two thieves,
And even one of them began to believe.

You see, it's never too late to be saved.
Study Christ's life and the way He paved.
And when we take holy communion,
We should all think in unison
About that night when Jesus and His disciples met.

That is an event we should never forget.
They consumed the bread and wine—
Which represented His broken body and His blood
divine.
He then went on to meet the fate
That God the Father had written on His slate.

Even though He died that day, He arose and still He lives.
We can tell He holds no grudge by all the blessings He gives.
Although it's impossible to be just like Him,

We should try to be more Christlike – it doesn't happen on a whim.
We should read the Bible, pray, praise Him, and love one another,
And treat everyone as if they were our own mother,
father, sister, or brother.
Be cheerful, sing a song, and thank Him every day.
As merciful and kind as God is, we'll be well on our way
To a full, fruitful, and happy life—
Not one filled with lots of heartaches, toil, and strife.
We're not perfect, so we must ask for forgiveness.
This is just the Christianly order of business.

So as we celebrate this Easter time of year,
Along with the new outfits, chocolates, jelly beans, and cheer,
Remember that our Savior sacrificed His life… and died on Calvary
For everyone on this earth, including ME.

CHAPTER SEVEN

TICKLED TO BE ALIVE ...

STAYING AFLOAT/MAINTAINING

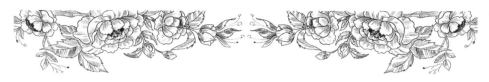

MOST WANTED

A world full of peace, love, and harmony,
A beautiful place for you and for me,
People of all races getting along,
Able to distinguish right from wrong.

Caring, sharing, and lending a helping hand,
Giving that little extra whenever you can,
Showing our youth the right way to go,
Imparting knowledge, teaching respect and other things they
need to know,

Uplifting and applauding our seniors, thanking God for their
        presence,
Making them feel special – and enjoying their effervescence.
Feeding the hungry with our abundance of food
And helping the homeless will surely brighten their moods.

Enjoying the beauty of places far and near,
Counting our many blessings throughout the year,
Recognizing just how precious life is,
Honoring and glorifying the Supreme Being – all of this is His.

These are all the things I want most
All things are possible – let's try a dose!

FORGIVENESS

One of the ways to live a good life
And to avoid unnecessary strife
Is to learn how to forgive—
And God will show you how to live!

Being unforgiving can be such a burden.
It weighs you down and keeps you hurtin'.
Pray to God to help you let go.
Surrender to Him and watch HIS blessings flow.

Forgiveness doesn't mean forgetting,
But it does prevent you from letting
Satan control your actions and mind,
Keeping you from being kind.

Unforgiveness causes more harm
And keeps you from showcasing your charm.
So free up all those negative emotions.
Replace them with positive daily devotions.

Life is too short to waste precious time.
Being unforgiving can rob you blind.
So surely, now, you will agree
You'd much rather feel free and filled with glee.

Forgive and remove that internal ugly beast—
And watch the Power of Forgiveness give you peace!

IT'S YOUR CHOICE!

Love versus anger or hate?
God and the Bible say love is great!

Do you have faith, or are you always full of fear?
Believe and depend on God, for HE makes it very clear!

Are you forgiving or do you practice unforgiveness?
Don't carry a grudge – He's forgiven us!

Smile, sadness, or wearing a frown?
Smiles are uplifting, while a long face brings you down!

Generosity versus holding back?
Choosing stinginess over giving is certainly whack!

There's no contest between imprisonment and being free.
To lie is to die! So why?

The truth will set you free – this we can all plainly see!

Pride over gratitude?
You better check your attitude!

Spirit over flesh?
If you choose flesh, you really are a mess!

So, in this life—
There will be much strife.
Many choices will have to be made—
But, for our sins, His life He gave.

Form a relationship with HIM!
Before your light goes dim.
Do the right thing with your voice—
MAKE SURE YOU MAKE THE RIGHT CHOICE!
God bless!

CHAPTER EIGHT

TICKLED TO BE ALIVE ...

PUSHING AHEAD

KEEP ON PUSHING

Keep on pushing and never quit.
For when you do, you surely go back a bit.
God has promised to never leave our side.
Love and accept Him, and, in you, He will always abide.
No matter the circumstances, don't give up.
Keep on pushing like a determined little pup.
God is bigger than anything you will ever face.
Lean and depend on Him – He will help you win the race.
Remember, the devil comes to kill, steal, and destroy,
But through God, there is victory, hope, peace, and joy.
His grace and mercy follow you every day of your life.
He will help you overcome negativity and all kinds of strife.
Trust and have faith in God. You can't do it by yourself.
Surrender to Him – you definitely need His help.
So I'm here to encourage you. Don't be a quitter!
Doing things through Christ surely makes you a winner.

KEEP, ENJOY, OR LET GO!

People come, and people go.
The question is… how should you know?

Certain come just for a reason.
Others come just for a season.
Then, there are those who are around forever,
Through thick and thin or any kind of weather.

Life is full of many surprises.
Only God knows for sure, cuz He is the wisest.
When we love for a reason, we give and get love.
When it's seasonal, look for guidance from above.

When people come into your life…
Your relationship with God can protect you from strife.
He'll help you guard your heart and minimize damage.
He's always there for you and will help you manage.

He'll guide you in loving reasonably
And show you whether it should only be seasonally.

So the moral of the story that you should know:
God will show you whether to keep, enjoy, or to let go!

LOSS OF A LOVED ONE

Although your loved one is physically gone,
Hopefully, your grieving will lessen as time moves on.

God is our Comforter and certainly knows best.
HE decided to call them home for some much-needed rest.
Feel blessed to have spent many years together,
Filled with ups and downs, but mostly happiness.

Be thankful for all the good traits they had.
Focus on the memories that make you feel glad.
Think about the good ways they made an impact.
Their inner beauty was quite evident – that's a fact.

Be thankful for the love and support of
family and friends who care.
Help them with the sadness and grief that they too share.
Hope that in your time, you can begin to move on
Through prayer and perhaps some
insightful words from a song.

Your heart is broken today and for years to come,
But your spirit and theirs will forever connect as one.

Just remember to keep God first and let HIM lead the way.
HE loves and will strengthen you day by day.

CHAPTER NINE

TICKLED TO BE ALIVE ...

SHOUT-OUTS

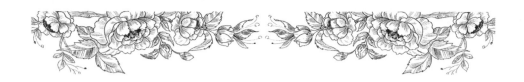

DON'T BE SHY. GIVE BALTIMORE A TRY!

Baltimore is on the East Coast of the United States,
And its large size makes Maryland rate.
Two hundred miles from the Atlantic, near
the mouth of Chesapeake Bay,
There are lots of things to do to help you plan your stay.
Over 600,000 people call Baltimore home,
With over 4,000 acres of parkland to roam.

Yes, Baltimore is one of America's finest cities.
Why, a trip here will leave you feeling quite witty.
"Charm City" is Baltimore's famous nickname.
Its historical attractions and the Inner
Harbor are its claims to fame.
Its fine restaurants, shopping, and quaint neighborhoods,
The many museums, theaters, and fine
hotels are just some of the goods.

There are many schools and universities galore—
And the Baltimore Ravens boast eye-catching scores.
The Aquarium, Science Center, and World Trade Center,
The Zoo, Oriole Park, and Port Discovery are all winners.

There are many interesting shops in Fell's Point.
Also located, there are some real jazzy joints.
The beautiful skyline has many buildings
standing so tall and still,
And south of the harbor, you'll find historic Federal Hill.

Little Italy contains places serving good food.
They surely will put you in an excellent mood.

In this area, you will engage in endless outings
Because there are so many beautiful surrounding counties.

So, if you are looking for a place that's really neat,
This city will sweep you off your feet.
So why don't you consider paying this place a visit?
For the City of Baltimore can be quite exquisite!

 GET OUT OF HERE, CORONA!

Get out of here, Corona. We have had enough!
You have created lots of havoc, and we're tired of your stuff!

We were going about our lives, living day to day—
Then you came along in such a devastating way!
You refer to yourself by many names, including COVID-19.
You brought our activities to a screeching
halt. You are oh so mean!

Before you came, we were so carefree, wheeling and dealing.
Now, we've sheltered in place so long,
we're not sure how we're feeling.

We're stuck wearing masks, social distancing,
and constantly washing our hands,
And you made us say goodbye to all our previously made plans.
Many don't feel safe going out… not even going to church.
I tell you, Corona, or whatever you call
yourself, you're a piece of work!

Jobs have been lost and businesses closed—
There are so many things that are out of control.
Gone are the days of socializing, traveling, and doing what we do.
We're isolated, scared, and so confused;
some days, we don't have a clue.
You came on the scene with all your
madness and changed all the rules.
There's lots of sickness and tragic deaths,
and they closed the schools.

But all is not lost, and I'm here to say
Believe and be thankful, for God will have His way!

May I suggest to my comrades spending
time spreading love, joy, and peace,
Praying and being hopeful that this
pandemic will eventually cease,
We should do some things that we have put off for a while
And make relaxing and resting a part of our new style.

Keep the faith, take care of ourselves,
and use common sense.
Counting our blessings, trusting in God, and
worrying less should make us less tense.
Doing these things will decrease the times
that might make us just wanna
Throw up your hands and join me in
shouting, "Get out of here, Corona!"

TICKLED TO BE ALIVE, PART II

Tickled to be alive – such a happy saying!
It makes me thankful, puts pep in my step,
and makes me feel amazing.
A phrase I have been saying for so many years,
It usually produces good feelings, smiles, and never tears.
It makes me focus on the good more than the bad.
It highlights my blessings and the best experiences I have ever had.

Generally, I maintain a happy and even disposition,
Although life's "stuff" can sometimes alter my position.
But I am blessed by the best, and He has been so good to me.
So, I give Him all honor and praise and am filled with much glee.

God's so loving, forgiving, merciful, and gives lots of grace.
He has provided all I need to run life's long race.
He comforts, strengthens, and displays much kindness.
He gives peace, joy, and plenty of happiness.
He helps me show the love in my heart.
He encourages me to do my part.

Hopefully, some of the positive things in my book
Uplift, inspire, or make you take another look.

Draw closer to God while you still have time,
For I can attest, He is a good friend of mine.
Don't let the evil one put you in the dumps,
Keeping you looking sad or like you've got the mumps.

Enjoy life, be grateful, stand up and cheer.
You're tickled to be alive. Show it. Shout it loud and clear!

CONCLUSION

That brings us to the end of my first book! It is my hope that my poems, affirmations, spiritual nuggets, or other things have encouraged, enlightened, or energized you to become closer to God.

The gift of life that God has given us should not be taken lightly. He wants us to have and enjoy an abundant life. We have had or will experience many life lessons, and it is my hope that this book helps you to recognize how amazingly awesome God is and reminds you how grateful we should be for His unconditional love and the many blessings He provides.

Remember, He is always with us and will never leave or forsake us. Some days, we may experience fun and laughter, and then there may be days filled with some sorrow or pain. But, through both good times and bad, we must be thankful, trust and depend on Him, and continue pressing onward through this journey called life.

With God, all things are possible, and you too can be "Tickled to Be Alive" and enjoy life where you are, and on the way to where you are going.

God bless!

REFERENCES